SPECIAL SUBCOMMITTEE

Special Subcommittee

SAMUEL SOLOMON

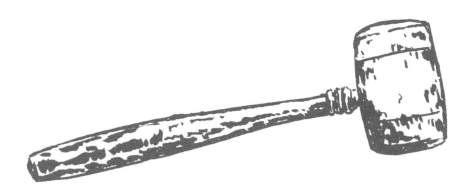

∞

Commune Editions
Oakland, California
communeeditions.com

An imprint of AK Press / AK Press UK
Oakland, California (akpress@akpress.org)
Edinburgh, Scotland (ak@akedin.demon.co.uk)

Commune Editions design by Front Group Design
    (frontgroupdesign.com)
Cover illustration by Amze Emmons
Library of Congress Cataloging-in-Publication Data 2017936130

Solomon, Samuel
    Special Subcommittee / Samuel Solomon.
    ISBN 978-1-934639-23-8 (pbk.: alk. paper)

Printed on acid-free paper by McNaughton & Gunn, Michigan, U.S.A.   The paper
    used in this publication meets the minimum requirements of ANSI/NISO Z39.48-1992
    (R2009)(*Permanence of Paper*).

TABLE OF CONTENTS

Sonnet

Does everyone here hurt each
other who loves anything of me?
If you do, I don't mind—
I'll love me more.

When you say you want
to run your tongue
up my receding gums—
When you just do it.

What we're trying to do is write the songs that
give the rhythm for a march that isn't here.
When you're already doing it, give me a beat
to keep it up and get down to it best.

We'll build it outside song, see if the song
I've also built holds on.

Feelings

(for Emma Heaney)

We're going to the party why are all these people here?
They're all different kinds of people wait no they are all the same
We spent the day a-marchin' and now we are at the bar.
This bro needs a good neck punch cuz he has no good ideas
About how to get the speaker to the soundsystem. I'm transported
In front of it, am not sure how, and this banner is twisting everywhere
Because it has three different posts. I can't be bothered to explain,
But it was really hard to carry and we're trying to move fast
Among the other moving people. It's much simpler in the bar
To cut vertically thru your teeth with a laser than it is to
Beam the day back up. I'm relieved by some suspension for
I've often described these novelistic feelings but never
Sought to change them. The last thing I wanted was to bring
It to the bar, to explain it to nonpartisans who drink up
Our blood like Manhattans. They could have been there, too,
Or no, they couldn't. Emma, kick me in the pants again,
And tell me why I'm wrong; you wouldn't smile unless
You meant it. I pick friends apart from others and we
Just pick friends apart. All day you were becoming ferocious
But it wasn't a very good protest and this is certainly not a good
Bar and we're getting careless now but talking, we are trying.
You photograph yourself crying and open the little curtain
And yell Hey, get in here, and I get it. I'm tired now I'll rest my head

On the last thing I want to tell you. I tell you by not telling.
Waiting at the bar now a small forward's all I am, but
Waiting at the curbside might just make the day stop leaving.

chaparral song

i can't stop leaning on you like a hug, jerked
on its foundation—i have become a balance beam.

i hate my love-me pants and words—
you pivot and sidestep the pine plank—*mine*.

        ✳ ✳   ✳

i've measured them from night to night:
tiny ponds of splooge gleam in hawk-stripped light.

Alexander doesn't want to be a warrior, so he fights back. Fight out the distance from honor to charm: find out the answer is Klingon love bomb.

That tooth-baring sectarian grin is fleshy, gleaming, trained right into my nipples, I think, though I keep turning back to catch their eyes with my exaggerated, gawking WHAT right there where expression fails, where public speech and backroom dealing, snark and smiles are the same, where talk can just disclose betrayals, where we have nothing to do with each other but betray, where this is the only moment that they'll look at me at all. And this is what it looks like to work together.

I speak out into what just hugs as delegate for its vanishing reputation. Now all that is gone enough. It's all too pat, what we already know, but each time it's different, and sometimes it's worse. When I'm nervous and feeling most like crap that's when I turn on the charm offensive with a bad kind of effeminacy, presto swagger trauma for impostor impression management. I can still get by on charm, flaunt a big smile right back. Alexander doesn't want to be a warrior, so he fights back.

Mildfire

It will have nothing to do with this
but imagine: this body modifies
silicates. Burns coil and
ostracism shards.

It's watching writing flee the city's
slate and flint for hand-built ashes.
It's watching clay hold shapes,
conduct, and watching what kills

hold its own shape. It's not polite
to stare, but between licks of shame
& defiance it's as close to right as
I know to look. A killing gesture

shapes its own world, sharpness
tosses this one off, even some
statements smash the whole heap
I've made of greenware beads.

1980s!

what you have is a void
that walks me backward, and the
church steps in my place.
What I have is relief
that you have long legs, too.

I've been workin' in the superstructure
writing to the press too long
with what I think I can't say
to the party or won't but then will, and do.

The city was at least fifty percent racist then and
now it's all more housing lies or sex-class and,
worse, people-class—

you know more about me than
about the jargon I take on
in the name of science.
O, 1980s, change that, please!

spring open us

caught rehearsing inanities
 like confrontational happiness

that worry is
 what makes me one
  with frankly sexual rhetoric
                    swaddled
                      dragging
                       strings
                      stability
                      in rows
                       of speaking
                      slings

clean and jerk and reinflate
 our metric tantrum chanting
  bread and roses in the street
   snot love snot hate, depreciate.

backstroke flags, be truthful
 there's bad stuff out there
  show some appreciation of complaint—

She Drives the Buick

How do your queer Marxist poets propagate?
Come back to certain names with variations
to indicate the revulsion-complex, so
attraction, coolness, etc. of that person
her *famous* actions, sense of an unhinging
contingently controls her fame, made
necessary somehow. Then notice how the gay
bitch's verge wilts down into radical queer.

Little Miss Manning's a rich snobby old lady
she threatened to throw a glass of rosé in my face
but quickly remembered her delicacy and simply
snickered she'd out me on the internet…pointing
                                    like Maleficent—
(she knows me, she walked with me once upon a dream,
in fact in a childhood *nightmare* featuring a witch
who was also a wasp, counting children with her
sinister hand, stinging-finger pointed, what could be
more terrifying than counting children well I'm
scared!)—like Maleficent, then, we toss
each other heaps of appropriated shade, I mean,
what kind of man is *that*. I know you're thinking
this too, and that says most about me. We want
to be Miss Manning *and* the witch.

unfruitable

Let's find the diamond days of boys and chatter,
tongues that slime from chewing on fruit leather
cooled down to a calmer state of matter,
chewed and spat out into hotter weather.

Or, prolapsed pandas falling from the sky:
they'll beg for downtime from their cruel procedure,
to stay with us while we get wet and dry,
and please to keep them even if by seizure.

It's there with mitts and paws in heaps of sand
that many creatures seek out something fast.
Between the breakers foam catches my hand,
and nipple-biting fish make a dark mast.

But we like beaches cleaner than our streets,
and fish too seldom crawl up in our sheets.

It Happened

It's a currency in language to have at it still and stronger;
and now folks are working harder than a dormouse to end hunger.
These rudiments of polis come in fact later and longer,
though their prescience felt originary ruse or still much wronger,

if not still higher, well then it's still calibrated, *camper*,
and something quite specific bangs and bellows through the damper,
and slower still but never still it sneaks into my hamper
so laundry time brings back what was encrusted 'neath the Pampers.

Well ok baby Uncle Sam's returned happy to bring you
books, nightlights, and blankets, make it easier to sing you.
Feeling bubbly when I'm called out so to say after disaster
that I never meant for loss to turn out vengeful so much faster

than the loss only imagined had it coming—*all* I'd tell them.
Now the moths are stuck to walls; they leave brown dustprints on the vellum.
Beyond beauty, then, they whirr, 'til wrenched together into packets
then uncloaked and crushed to powders smacked and sprayed out of our racquets.

Document 1

Let's be clear: the headliner is the document. This is not a polemic; it's the volume of a history smashing what little I chose to say. I have at times witnessed the crime of lyric fluency, and now I'd better prawn up to being a serious person. My utter indifference is not even a decent lie. Try again: it's something, quite, to apprehend so many details and their interrelations. Is that documentary? No more questions, each a way to be struck dumb, and there are many, and many interject. Instead, I will be wowed by an orchestra, neither didactically appreciating what a disciplined collective can achieve horizontally nor fearing its implementation by force.

it's not that this is testament to some great excess of what is
but that we are undeserving of that gory story that left centuries
to the side as aberrations or latencies. I can muster a happy
birthday smile through the tremendous anxiety at being
wrong and at that having no consequences, which is not so far off
from packing to go on a mid-length trip, now figure those pragmatics.

now I'll incorporate your critique

                                               yum yum yum yum

now another parent's permission consoles now I'll take this one for truth
now I am biting off a one-man strike and slurring the global chatter
with the wrong papers to inherit it all unlegislated, even my DNA is an
FBI file and some kindhearted memories never mine for telling were
extra-legally digitized and now all the decades have gone down the shore

A paper trail of
trail of nothing.
show shows they
what they're
really, how many
calls can you get
mean, "it is noted
semester begins
the second week
Someone actually
the secret files
agency. From now
my eyes I'll know

the subject's neighboradvised that the subject a
his family are away for the summer…said she did
not know where they were but she believed them
to have rented a cottage in Rockaway, Queens,
NY, and will probably return when the regular
school semester begins…. It is noted that the
school semester begins approximately the second
week in September and since the present address
of the subject is unknown, efforts to interview the
subject will not be made until the second week
in September or until it is ascertained that the
subject has returned to his permanent residence

nothing. A paper
What they'll
have no idea
doing. I mean
pretext phone
shouted out of. I
that the school
approximately
in September."
wrote that in
of a government
on when I close
the provenance

of each part and stick to that. It's like sheet music, but orchestration may no longer mean
anything if we can just rush the stage: now imagine the slaughter. Do you picture this like
the symphony or like you're in a dark-green vinyl La-Z-Boy with your eyes closed? That's
more vivid, but I can't make either for you. It's just a metaphor, after all, and I'm still
young; I've got to hang out first.

Document 2

Thirty-five years later send a third-generation
request, at least we'll say we're sending it, it's probably
the same FBI shit: purely conceptual writing. Looking for
a really human sign in these redactions is risible,
no matter that someone probably scared stiff
and also living did this, too. My issue is a redder
shout: an older red and lines bled out of broader
strokes in just facades of struggle and an inverse
tedium called documentary, called FBI file
for family history. Make the dead quaint or else sprout
the tedious details, opaque facts of descent
and these ridiculous feelings of scholarship.

Here's an axiom: there is no possibility for anything called revolutionary inheritance. Which
is not the same thing as ancestry but which is the dominant constitution of reproduction all

how can we line? And what that indicate? A lyric line slides lamentation syllable but inches long. that middle forbidden from got some hazy gered like "the you'll sense I in mind. I no *idea*, but "something" is *like* lying but aloud, it rather acting. I mean, But the line isn't at all. When I

[Name redacted] furnished information on January 29, 1958 which certified that NATHAN SOLOMON was issued IWO Certificate Number 24008 in Lodge Number 138 in May, 1939; was transferred to Lodge Number 607 on an unknown date; was expelled on March 1, 1947; was reinstated in June, 1947; was expelled in March, 1948; was reinstated in April, 1948; was expelled in September, 1948; was reinstated in October, 1948; was expelled in September, 1949; was reinstated in December, 1949; was expelled in September, 1950; was reinstated in March, 1951 and paid through September, 1953. According to this information, SOLOMON was born on March 21, 1910 in Russia. At the time of his application he resided at 436 Fort Washington Avenue and was employed as a union organizer. The IWO has been designated by the Attorney General of the United States pursuant to Executive Order 10450

the same. So reproduce a kind of line does proposition: the too easily into if it's over one less than three From now on range will be verse. Now I've sense of lyric fin-sense." Maybe have something certainly have that's not what means. Lyric isn't it; still, read resembles bad "Line, Please?" waiting, it isn't

Peculiarities

Has small mustache (width of nose)

say "I'm writing" what I'm doing is saying that I'm not doing some other thing. And I can't ever do it the same (not doing, that is) but it's still samey. The banal sheerness of washed out light is fallacious but not pathetic. No, it's affective but not fallacious, really it might name a set of coinciding or distinct

Document 3

That's a nice tank you've rolled in on and that's not a metaphor for life but it's in it, in it, in life. I wonder about your chariot service-worked into your hands by rusted association. Writing to you is one way to focus, so here's it all *at work*, you see the work makes it figure better instead. When low-riding, time flirting, yeah, drive by me It would seem was requested 1948. Who was Folks from the bosses? For all I this because you

The subject was contacted for interview by Bureau Agents on 10/14/54. The subject was quite hostile and refused to talk with the agents. From a review of the subject's case file there is no reason to believe that the subject would cooperate with Bureau Agents at this time. Further, since he is in the printing business, it is possible that a contact with him could prove embarrassing to the Bureau. Therefore, no interview with the subject is recommended at this time.

it's well past for drive-by these accidents all the time. that the file before, in seeking it out? union, or the know, you read have to. That

thought cleanses me just as I try to mess it up. That thought sanitizes my nervous soul, makes it *contemporary music*, and the public beats are jogging in my head. I'll be anything but anodyne or ponderous or I'll say something else, some simple truth. I'll be a structural, nonhuman, public rhythm.

Who has never been on or in some special subcommittee?
My family is another one, so an easy analogy frames
the work. This family is congressional.
A precarious form, this tendency, a fraction, faction,
internal opposition, a wing, what whole does it
express or conceal? *or does it explode?*
Is it the whole of Congress, then?
Now I need another mind to synthesize mine,
another you to get us off that island.
You want me to say it all. Every time.
Repeat every truth I've already shown.
It's not that I still know it, not saying it,
but I might want to do something else now.
I'll bro it up at someone's house and
find a man to get the best of me.
Form another committee and then learn
Why Men Pull Away.

Explanation of exemptions (b)(7)(E)
investigatory records compiled for law
enforcement purposes, the disclosure
of which would disclose investigative
techniques and procedures, thereby
impairing their future effectiveness.

Document 4

It would seep downward — not upward, top-down metaphors are correct here — into every interaction, so that when they imagined their three minutes at the bullhorn they couldn't decide if they were as angry about the useless interaction in the hallway with a coworker

as they
the direct
on 'civil
they were
fact that they
this at all, to
were about
they could
as a choice,
about the fact
ecumenical
that remain
as they were

The subject was contacted at his residence on 10/14/54, by SAS [redacted] and [redacted]. The subject appeared at the peephole in the door of his apartment. Before the agents could advise the subject the purpose of the contact the subject said, through the peephole, "I know who you are. I have nothing to say." SA [redacted] identified the agents by showing his commissioned card to the subject, through the peephole, while at the same time he was attempting to clarify the purpose of the contact. At this point the subject closed the peephole and was heard to walk away from the door. The interview was terminated at this point. It is noted regarding the subject's attitude that he was quite hostile to the agents.

were about
impingement
liberties,' as
about the
had to do
work, as they
the fact that
perceive this
as they were
in solidarities
cloistered,
about the

fact that their anger could even possibly be a matter for contemplation, as they were about the utter irrelevance of their struggles against civility, as they were about the fact that their comforts were private, as they were about the fact that their intimacies are hidden, as they were about the possibility that they might be forced to be public instead, as they were about the fact that writers think they can produce meaning alone, as they were about the fact that they believed this, as they were about the fact that the rhythms of anger seem especially irreducible to description

Right now I want my life back. Another time I didn't. I wanted it over there, but now I want it here. No, not here; here is where I'm not listening to this and wanting it back over there.

Let's sweep some things around this little room so we can keep on living it alone, unmolested and thoroughly private facing the life out there which is your only one, but that's not true.

You have the room so you can close a door and do what?

You've kept my bed, and the door is open. Your rhythm and your penis meet on my wrist for a sense of the man I'm sure I am not: but have I got a wife? You might have a wife I am not it, though; I'm not one.

Now the door is off its hinges.

Ask the really gay question: dorsal fuck?

But no one does it like you. Instead, inside
the consoling effect, they'll see themselves
against the matter, swagger,
and if there's smoke in solitude, still
I'm a stomach with two sets of legs
and a hand—teaching in track pants—
and how much I talk, to bring a hand,
to remind me, to the feet,
of my gayest reliance on me.

Complexion	Medium sallow
Height	5 feet 5 inches to 6 feet
Build	Short and heavy

Document 5

I don't need to tell you the story; you already know it. The whole thing will be yours (a different you, now), directed at you, my in-law. I'm ready to let it rip, and you'll do. Feeling becomes another person: a comfortable queer with sperm. The feeling is rage. I have nowhere to put it, so it's here. If you say the wrong word, you will be the problem. The moment is that of seeing the impersonal structure can still hit you with an identity category *and* a behavior simultaneously and make you circle "heterosexual" and "no" in order to continue.

One of us is in the sun.

One of us is thinking about the sun but is not in it.

Both of us have been together in the sun.

I take your life, I give you none.

Your hand impressions:

I have them on file.

I make no impressions.

I make no images.

My hands were on very little the day that I was heterosexual. Not only but also a disori-
enting rage where the big picture is easy but real even so. I'll tell because I can't show
it —there's a way in which it's obvious and then also indirect, absurd— that the state will
sanction, that private industry will profit from this so that the middle income queer person

with sperm is
off-scene, can-
to share fluids
sphere where
from what
private. But it
rage directed at
a simple social
abstraction:
your body as I
your hand on

[Redacted] of known reliability, advised in July 1950
that the automobile registered to the subject was seen
in the main parking lot of Camp Lakeland, Sylvan
Lake, Hopewell Junction, New York on July 4, 1950.
According to [redacted] of known reliability, Camp
Lakeland-Camp Kinderland are located at Sylvan
Lake in the vicinity of Hopewell Junction, New
York and are two camps in one: Camp Lakeland
being for adults and Camp Kinderland for children.

weirdly thrown
not be permitted
in the public
profits are made
must be kept
still ends in my
another person:
realism, a real
my in-law. I miss
write this. I miss
my arm while I

lean on your lap. You hold my hand: will it keep holding the pen or will it drop? You hold
my hand as it holds the pen, (you can't hold my hand if I'm typing, which I'm not), but you
hold the pen with me —so that I write so happy I can drop it. Without your hand I will rage
and stew and be attached to those feelings, seek revenge, fantasize screaming at my in-law
who is the law as far as I'm concerned today, and today can last a long time

Document 6

I didn't know my paternal grandfather very well, which is to say that I still don't. I sometimes ask for stories about him, the same ones, filtered through, what else, my dad's love, anger, disappointment, self-protection, and a sort of loyalty, though I'm not sure to what, exactly. That's one strand in the history of racial formation—the family as committee might be a different one. A totally bureaucratic intimacy, since a truly democratic centralist organization of kinship would be a category error. A grouping of affinities would probably be, too. These forms cross over and do not answer for each other or much else. And I cannot even ask the questions that impel me, not even enough to fail—fragments never do—and collages won't cut it. A gay international that's not very international at all. I did, however, know my grandmother:

The subject's wife BETTY SOLOMON (NY file 100-76838) was recommended for interview. It is noted that the subject's wife BETTY SOLOMON, NY file 100-76838, was interviewed on 4/23/54. She displayed a very hostile and uncooperative attitude advising that she would furnish no information to the FBI about anything.

That sounds about right. Of course, she was a party member herself, but I don't have her file. So the patronymic reasserts its force. I repeat it: I am not, do not have, a wife. This is my inadequation. In both cases, there is a certain work of unknowing, attempting to generate some other knowledge through both my own cuts and the redactions of government documents supplemented by fragments of "my life": my activities and passions, the worlds I inhabit and those I would just like to inhabit. But this is not an honest attempt at totality on the level of a psychological or social realism – this is also not *The Golden Notebook*, for reasons of necessity and inadequacy. I have stories, and I have some research skills, and I also have an incomplete oral history conducted by my cousin. These don't really fill in gaps, if we're being honest. I don't really want them filled in, I should say: I suture them with my doctrinal leanings, pressed in and out of shape, by, well, "form," understood here as the contingent forces of circumstance. The point was to write a set of mini essays on "the family" in order to document the cynical attachments that come from a fear of loneliness and to understand how I have the capacity to cry from watching *Homeland*. Meanwhile, there's a part of the file where Special Agent [redacted] gets in some trouble for his failure to submit a report about my grandfather's case. An explanation for this is requested by the higher-ups, and his scrambling excuse is printed right in the file—he claims that no one had actually asked him to submit the report—as are the notes from his Supervisor insisting that indeed his subordinate "SA [redacted] was personally instructed to proceed with the investigation of this case." There's a different kind of subject captured here, this agent on file, and I can hate him. But I can also feel his shame: it still does its mammalian tingling.

HEARINGS

BEFORE A

SPECIAL SUBCOMMITTEE OF THE
COMMITTEE ON EDUCATION AND LABOR
HOUSE OF REPRESENTATIVES

EIGHTIETH CONGRESS

SECOND SESSION

PURSUANT TO

H. Res. 111

(80th Congress)

HEARINGS HELD AT WASHINGTON, D. C., JUNE 30,
JULY 1 AND 2, AUGUST 3, 4, 10, AND 11, AND AT
NEW YORK, N. Y., JULY 7, 8, AND 9, 1948

SPECIAL SUBCOMMITTEE TO INVESTIGATE COMMUNISM IN NEW YORK
CITY DISTRIBUTIVE TRADES

CHARLES J. KERSTEN, Wisconsin, *Chairman*

FRED A. HARTLEY, JR., New Jersey   JOHN LESINSKI, Michigan
CARROLL D. KEARNS, Pennsylvania   JOHN F. KENNEDY, Massachusetts
                                 JOHN S. WOOD, Georgia

JOHN O. GRAHAM, *Investigator*

TESTIMONY OF NATHAN SOLOMON, PRESIDENT, LOCAL 830, RETAIL
AND WHOLESALE EMPLOYEES UNION, NEW YORK, N. Y.

The court failed to protect me
at home. He called my folks to say
I was not needed, but it was a secret
in the first place not offered for truth

but for a reasonable person a cause of
harm made analysis suggest cash
flow. Compared to that D.A. I can
forgive matters of scale.

Is that called maturity, futility
or senility? Serenity is just
one part of the prayer; there's also
a bit about rage that's pertinent enough
not to worry my lack of beauty.

Mr. KERSTEN. Are there a number of contracts presently in negotiation or have you got them pretty well all closed up, or what is the situation?

Mr. SOLOMON. Well, some of our contracts are in negotiation and some have been concluded. We are at the present time involved in a couple of very serious strikes insofar as our local union is involved; and, as a matter of fact, we feel that this investigation is in a sense prejudicing our ability to win these strikes. We believe that this investigation plays into the hands of management and encourages them to resist our efforts to get the wages and working conditions for which our members are striving. There are a number of contracts which are also due at about this time and, apparently, from all indications given to me the managements of these companies are hoping that this investigation might cause division and dissention in the ranks of our union and thereby aid them in trying to knock down the conditions which our members are justly entitled to get.

Well, hands strike as a matter of record.
Just strike hands *well* as a matter of
fact. Well—used as an interjection and an
expression of surprise—this is nothing to say
compared to just rewritten surprise.

Well, what is the situation, rank it well, come
in my catheter, I mean cathedral, say
"colostomy bag," and try to collect, I mean *organize*
the nurses. Always sing "Joe Hill" well.

I remember very little. Ranks were closing—hands join
now—it was embarrassing. I was eleven and my father's
knuckles were all busted from fighting
thugs. Was he one? There is a lot that I don't
know holding them now.

Mr. KERSTEN. Has your local or the officers of your local signed the non-Communist affidavit so as to qualify under the NLRB?

Mr. SOLOMON. Well, the officers of our union have been instructed by our membership at various meetings to bypass the Taft-Hartley board and to refuse to comply because of the dubious benefits that might be gotten. As a matter of fact, the Taft-Hartley board and the act make it difficult for unions to secure the benefits and conditions which our members seek to obtain, and our membership at various meetings have decided that they would prefer that we seek to secure our benefits without utilizing the board or any sections of the law. And as a matter of fact, we believe that we can successfully secure wages, hours, and other working conditions for our membership precisely because we don't get entangled in the red tape and the long delays and other procedures that the National Labor Relations Board as presently constituted forces unions to get involved in. As a matter of fact, our membership has by experience found that this present National Labor Relations Board has made it possible for employers to company-unionize their stores, to bring in unions which are not the choice of the workers, to seek elections at a time when there are no contests or real disputes, but to actually provoke unions to step into the picture.

We have an experience, for example, in the Times Square auto-accessory store where the employer has actually brought a union, with a so-called label, into the picture, sought to unionize the antiunion elements, create division in the ranks of the union, and create the impression that there is a jurisdictional dispute when the only dispute is as to what wages, hours, and working conditions the workers should have.

members check the local workers board:
rank it well for the label's stay
in the picture. say store will not permit,
say *permit*, well it never files to strike
a local company union: small choices.

no system of two moieties, no grandmother
sacks fifth avenue compact
deal only in resource
metals can't end the fed in a surge

charging waves, gilt in old abundance, lords
and stewards secure store just in time
and wares permit ventures, each half life
over time dispute signed out with a punch

Mr. KERSTEN. Who were the speakers at this meeting?

Mr. SOLOMON. Well, there was myself as president of the union, and there were quite a number of rank and file workers right from the floor, who took the floor and discussed the questions....

Mr. KERSTEN. Did you start off the subject of accepting this report?

Mr. SOLOMON. I made the report, and it included a number of items in addition to the question of bypassing the Taft-Hartley board. But I discussed the question of our strikes, the need for our membership to recognize the obstacles being placed in our path by this antilabor legislation, and the need for reaffirming again the decisions made at previous meetings to go ahead and try to secure our conditions and benefits without reliance in any manner, shape, or form on the Taft-Hartley law; that in the event the law was used against us we would exercise all of our legal rights and remedies.

Mr. KERSTEN. Mr. Solomon, I asked if you made a speech; I didn't ask you to give it.... I will ask you one part of that speech. You did explain to them in the course of your speech why they shouldn't require the leadership to file the non-Communist affidavit?

Mr. SOLOMON. That is correct, sir.

File affidavit for the report board.
This is total admin people—
strike items from speech, rights from legal
meetings, claim items for law, strike
didactic anti-labor time is stricken.

Court reporters for the aristocracy of labor
want us to know the difference
between 7am and 9am between straight
time and overtime is the real opposite of straight
time not queer time but alien physics.

If you work part time you cannot be
excused from service, right, you can't
be most emphatic about everything—
not just that you don't want to work
at all and labor time is a dead end.

Mr. KERSTEN. So at least that night the members didn't more or less initiate the subject and request the leadership to take certain actions?

Mr. SOLOMON. As a matter of fact——

Mr. KERSTEN. It was just the other way around.

Mr. SOLOMON. Let's be clear about that, sir. I don't believe that in any labor organization which has leadership the membership spontaneously tell the leaders what to do. The purpose of leadership is that they elect officers to give them guidance and advice, and that's our responsibility to come with suggestions and proposals, and to subject them to the examination of the membership, and that's precisely what we did and what we always do. Members are a morphous group. They elect bodies, just as Congress is elected, to pass laws. They elect the officers of the union in order to give guidance and cohesion to the program and policies of the union.

Mr. KERSTEN. I agree with your general thoughts on that subject that that's the purpose of leadership. But, did the members at any time, at any meeting, to your knowledge, initiate the discussion of whether or not the leadership should file non-Communist affidavits?

Authority to receive on behalf of
the rest—mass action the only weapon
institutes strategic necessity or
emotional need. Allegations of a
personality Antigone *could not be*

a social democrat on this showing
a perpetual opposition the only way to
be known and loved—at all costs—
neither sign nor receive checks on
anyone's behalf, always refuse office—

It was just the other way around, they
elect bodies to guide morphous bodies
to be a massive body. I agree with you
your general thoughts on that subject
that that's the purpose of leadership.

Mr. WOOD. Mr. Chairman, may I interrogate? As I understand it, Mr. Solomon, you made the report at this meeting?

Mr. SOLOMON. At the meeting of June 22?

Mr. WOOD. Yes.

Mr. SOLOMON. Yes.

Mr. WOOD. You submitted a report?

Mr. SOLOMON. Correct.

Mr. WOOD. And spoke in its favor?

Mr. SOLOMON. Well, if I made the report, I presume I was definitely in favor of it.

Mr. WOOD. I am asking you. You can answer that question "yes" or "no."

Mr. SOLOMON. It was my report; yes.

Mr. WOOD. And spoke in its favor?

Mr. SOLOMON. Well, I can't see any other thing that I could have done. It was my report. I was in favor of it because I made it.

Mr. WOOD. Well, will you please answer that question, then.

Mr. SOLOMON. Definitely.

submitted report bespoke a favor
may I interrogate? I made a report and spoke
in its favor, yes, definitely, I made it, yes,
it is my favorite, yes,

no report speaks for itself in its
interest. small business speaks "in our
favor" though retail extinction bespeaks
no question, skips a generation gap

between us, we can't get along any
more small retail shift-reports show
discrepancy in revenue and still no
mention is made of immigration policy

Mr. WOOD. You spoke in its favor, moved its adoption?

Mr. SOLOMON. No. The membership moved its adoption. I merely presented the report.

Mr. WOOD. Who moved its adoption?

Mr. SOLOMON. Some member from the floor took the floor and made a motion.

Mr. WOOD. And then you declared the result?

Mr. SOLOMON. No. We discussed it, sir.

Mr. WOOD. When the vote was taken, you declared the vote?

Mr. SOLOMON. After the vote was taken, certainly.

Mr. WOOD. You declared the result. So, if I get it correctly, then, everything was done there that night was done by you except somebody moved its adoption.

Mr. SOLOMON. I wasn't chairman of the meeting. I was only the reporter. The chairman of the meeting took the vote and opened the discussion. As a matter of fact, on the contrary, everything that was done at the meeting was done as a result of consultation with the membership of our union, starting with the executive council of the union, and resulting from discussion at the membership meeting. The meeting made certain divisions——

Mr. WOOD. I wanted to get it clear on the record.

Mr. SOLOMON. I assure you that I don't run the union as an individual. The membership runs our organization. We are a rank-and-file-membership union. As a matter of fact, one of the main planks at that meeting was that we encourage——

Mr. WOOD. We are not concerned with that.

Mr. SOLOMON. We encourage the membership to come to our meetings. We insist and, as a matter of fact, we made the central plank of that meeting that the membership participated fully in every meeting and in every organizational step of our union, and that's one of the——

Mr. WOOD. If you talk as much up there as you do here, how can anybody else say anything?

Mr. SOLOMON. Well, as a matter of fact, the floor is open for discussion, and there were dozens of members that took the floor. You are questioning me, so I presume I am on the floor, and I am required to talk.

However self-limited and vowed to
consultation and petty compromise
it is an audacious presumption for a
man to get into any position over his
fellows

                                  a central plank is the
right to trial by jury in postures
of "radical" inheritance everything
we believe could be contained in
the word feminist. get it clear on

the record not only moved for its
adoption but *required it to talk*
the floor into a discussion — in an
instant some member from the floor
took the floor and made a motion

Mr. KERSTEN. Mr. Solomon, just these questions. Will you state whether or not you are or ever have been a member of the IWO, International Workers Order?

Mr. SOLOMON. Sir, in view of the fact that I have been apprised in the newspapers and from various sources that that organization has been listed by Attorney General Clark, that that is a subversive organization, I wish to assert my constitutional rights on all provisions of the Constitution that pertain, and more particularly to the first and fifth amendments permitting freedom of association and permitting a witness not to incriminate himself. I believe that this question has no bearing whatsoever on the matter at hand and on our union and organization. I believe, sir——

Mr. KERSTEN. Just a minute.

Mr. SOLOMON. It is merely a method of prosecuting and persecuting us as witnesses.

Mr. KERSTEN. Just a minute, please. When I ask you to stop, I wish you would, please.

Mr. SOLOMON. I didn't understand that you meant me to stop.

Mr. WOOD. You can't understand a gavel?

Mr. KERSTEN. I don't see any——

Mr. WOOD. Are you as indifferent to your oath and all your other testimony as you were to that; that you don't understand the meaning of a gavel?

Mr. SOLOMON. I am not indifferent to my oath.

Mr. WOOD. Didn't you say that?

Mr. SOLOMON. I did not say that at all, sir.

Mr. WOOD. All right.

Mr. KERSTEN. I will order you to answer the question, Mr. Solomon, as to whether or not you ever have been or are now a member of the IWO, International Workers Order?

Mr. SOLOMON. I answered the question, sir, and I assert my constitutional rights.

oath meaning order pertaining to   GAVEL
testimony, rights, there is no equal
footing. associate member of state,
international organization with   GAVEL
I didn't understand I don't see any   GAVEL

no hearing loss in evidence
only memory, or a series of tests
and equalizing measures. hold yr nose
and blow smoke from yr blowhole
into contextless diagnostic air.

Shake hands with counsel and blow
oaths from every orifice with some
small business that has standing
orders still pertaining to a gavel
blow what if you meant me to stop

Mr. KERSTEN. I will ask you, Mr. Solomon, whether or not you ever were or are you now a member of an organization known as the Trade Union Committee to Free Earl Browder?

Mr. SOLOMON. I wish to assert my constitutional prerogative in respect to the fifth and first amendments, and any other constitutional provisions that might pertain thereto.

Mr. KERSTEN. And I order you to answer that question.

Mr. SOLOMON. I have answered it, sir.

Mr. KERSTEN. Mr. Solomon, I will ask you whether you ever have been or now are a member of an organization known as the Citizens Committee to Defend Representative Government which is an organization supporting the seating of the Communist Gerson?

Mr. SOLOMON. I wish to again assert, sir, that my constitution—I wish to again assert my constitutional rights under the first and fifth amendments of the Constitution and answer that question so.

Mr. KERSTEN. I will ask you have you ever been or now are a member of the Communist Party?

Mr. SOLOMON. I repeat my answer, sir, that I assert my constitutional rights concerning this question and, particularly, the first and fifth amendments of the Constitution.

Mr. KERSTEN. I order you answer this last question, Mr. Solomon, as to whether or not you ever were at any time or now are a member of the Communist Party.

Mr. SOLOMON. Sir, I believe that you are infringing on my constitutional rights; I assert them, and I believe that these questions do not pertain in any manner, shape, or form to the investigation of my duties as an officer of our union.

Mr. KERSTEN. Just a minute; just a minute.

Mr. SOLOMON. Regardless of their political belief.

false analogy between patriarchy
and state power is history, it's not
resemblance, not always the world
historical defeat of the female sex
but it also sometimes is just that

that affects the answers we can give,
rights we have inherited and skipped over,
dialectically reengaged some things
are not surprising, but still the best
response might be to strike inheritance

because males were less attached
to the matriarchal gens they began
to notice their own property, and
so it should be no surprise to you that
my originary myth ends in blacklist

Mr. KERSTEN. Just be quiet while the Congressman is talking.

Mr. WOOD. Is that the only answer that you are willing to give to that question, the one that you have given?

Mr. SOLOMON. Well, I will say again sir, that——

Mr. WOOD. Just answer that question "Yes" or "No"; is that the answer you are willing to give?

Mr. SOLOMON. I have given an answer.

Mr. WOOD. That is the only one you are willing to give?

Mr. SOLOMON I can elaborate on it if you wish, but that is the answer I have given.

Mr. WOOD. I do not want any elaboration; is that the only one you are willing to give?

Mr. SOLOMON. I am willing to give any answer which pertains to this investigation and that respects my constitutional rights.

Mr. WOOD. Is that the only answer you are willing to give to that question?

Mr. SOLOMON. I have given my answer.

Mr. WOOD. That is the only one you want to give?

Mr. SOLOMON. That is my answer, sir.

Mr. WOOD. That is all.

Mr. KERSTEN. You are excused.

Life of Riley

Invitations end in enjambment, doors
shut softly are no less indignant but
it never was dignity we're after.
>   The unsupported mothers group
>   is smart to squat as tactic but
>   the unsupported mothers group
>   was forced to squat as tactic and
>   that just might be true for longer
>   than it's interesting.
Fen access is restricted
to pastry thanks.

a fussy repose in being right
or in saying I was right
well there's a difference in it
        do note the eventual eviction
        by King's College from the house.
they laugh cuz they know they're untouchable
not because what I said was wrong

there are kinds of grasses

that you split open

down the middle

whistling anyway or

can't turn me away

i believe

in your heart.

but then you tell me

all our lies are also

knives, or else

your rectitude (I don't

mean mine), won't it

look shameful?

each is claiming material conditions
for the analytical framework there won't be proof
of what is really happening if I'm not there
may I still care whether you COME OR NOT

the real movement of history is also at and has
also been in the dead left which continues as material
force or only irrelevant reaction you would say that
I know you do all the time and then return to what

we all know so much
why DON'T we just write it down?
we probably do mean the leadership of the most
oppressed and not merely of the oppressed

workers and that fuckall anxiety about being right
is ours to share is a bad comfort he says
I hate it and love you but isn't it more
to hate the center since we don't all sin the same

windbag moneybags cat bag can bag
I too can rail against it and forsake it
in the interest of positions sometimes happy
at this point but not for blocks of fact

if I don't get a job will I walk my cat on a leash
neither doleful never when we'd rather compose

♪The world is full of Rileys
♪No matter what their name
I had some more pieces and lost them
naturally being a father in this hectic
world and coping with the problems
of teenage youth is a bewildering task
for even the most intelligent of us
some of us, you might need some comfort
and happiness so that we can struggle all
of us, you are already smashed to pieces
MUSIC: You still inspire me to write
poetry to you just the way you did on
our first DEATH-MARCH, INTO
TRANSITION And now, the American
Meat Institute brings you "The Life of Riley."
In a moment, we'll hear more of how
Riley handles his oncoming mother-in-law.
Take any mother-in-law. Scrape the in-law
off of her and what've you got? SUDDENLY
MILD this is Ken Niles speaking for meat.

Those people across an ocean,
where I reach for my talismanic tail.
That bar of metal that split my tongue,
it fell out in a casserole. Blossoming as
sustained, detailed practice. Perception
as meow. That dog as feathery, considered
not ontically but Veronically. But
not Veronical enough so

Read to me your lorries tale, sing to me your starfish, snail.
Tell me how *an oyster and clam aren't real family*
or there's not much to do when your friends are all fish

> OK stop singing
> now handsum
> cohabitation
> means consist
> in scarcity of
> sources
> > call me
> > fish.

They've confirmed that I am human in
this firefighter parking and
your concepts is a trap!
Give two-word answers and
re-read the text aloud. Refuse to explain.
    But up in his den—(Ah, my bachelor chum!)—
    But now is not to charm a chap
If I say we live there, I say I will not
For we live in the ghost of the old house now
    But now is not to charm a ghost

Not to make you feel it, if I could, as if
I did already anyway but in all the things
I might say if you were a chatbot who imagines
me thinking: that might not mean you think it.
You reject the premise, tap your fingers, groan and sigh.
        It's not easy to make
a fin of sense when I do break like a machine.
That's not everybody's femininity
to render unto you what's yours:
the dead goat made you vomit.

Reject the premise: the remainder will infuriate.
The premise is we live in the ghost of the old house
now your concepts is a trap, so I
give two-word answers and reread
the text aloud, refuse to explain
my accountability to my practice
is my petit bourgeois plan fucking b.

You were mean today, small-heart minded grouse,
you were oily of spirit. Let's reject
any rightness in friendship's small feelings,
neither can we speak those lines nor lie.
  But this is how it feels thinking toward you all the time,
    old Grandpa Scarecrow knows.
  I plead the fifth for you like him, like he.

Me, I've gone Babby in a grand BDS for
life, after all, is its ends. A common social
substance, you turn blue: It is the work,
it is the work detains. Stuff on, you
crystallize value, poised on the right
trope—click, turn, click— until
a choke stuck in your ears.

Right. It is the skin, it is the skin!
Pick any part and it's infected.
Poise of your nose reminded me of dad's.
He is not here he has outsourced the shadow of our right.
A party on the move is not often enough right.
These are not tactics raised to principles.
Every good poem is a transitional demand.

Pebble mine

Butchy cut-offs
tough and tumbling,
denim board shorts
with no apparent port,
facing into it split-lipped
and sprung without pastor,
pier and tower, wet sand cycling rollers
coast into the channel,
down into a cluck,
ducking rivers, sun developed,
orange cone, vermilion cape,
hot pink shoelace, too.

If memory serves me not at all
to unpack open conflict—
my room just set up, waiting
there for me to crawl back
and have that there and
not a home. My speaking matters
some in scale and solipsism's
trail not bad but binned with crab
meat bloated to mess up the
need beyond my tail—who cares

what brought me—here—
brought here, too, a body
broken by being a bridge.

It becomes reusable and I should never
speak to anyone on a Thursday
when it's like that
squeeze of the hand:
opened up to hug each part
by touch alone. It can also be
very simply not intense
or shattering, like sex can.
A fear was growing in my heart.
The fear grew sharper,
drawn away to where
there was no sun, but a sense of
external accomplishment:
look what I burped into me.
All that activity spruced out
of a need I don't want to mine.

A *quality of numbers*

                         lost the
code for my wardrobe
                         this
scarf shines the window
                         neck
curdling with flavors
                         I'm
snacking and savor
                         ing
eyes in the fire
                         place
smoke in the garden
                         my
rage in the shower
                         your
tears in the steam room
                         my
towel so heavy
                         your
mind is not like this
                         you're
patiently scheming
                         my
total demise and

you're

mad at me now cuz

my

one out of three is

your

three is enough so

what

more can you possi

bly

want you won't ask me

your

face is all flat and

my

habits are problems

your

anger is tumbling

my

feet into knobs and

my

face pays in hugs and

your

manifold rubbings

you're

two different folks who

tell

different stories

I

cannot remember

them

most of the time so

I

ask you again can

you

run down my thighs no

more

touching accounts of

a

life before mine and

my

opening up and

your

sullen expression
                    it
closes me down and
                    your
reddening weapons
                    are
killing me softly
                    with
horses.
shot in the arma
                    ment
socked in the faceplant
                    and
spending my balance
                    I'm
eating my fill with
                    no
middle for muscle
                    these
organs for keep

                    stop
kicking my ass at
                    this
round of the game you
                    don't
mean to deprive me
                    but
fabric forgives you
                    and
now I'm just burping
                    the
national anthem
                    for
curious jerkface
                    this
traveler's nervous
                    a
toilet for noble
                    men's
almost necessity.

learn how to sex on

       the

west coast

       a longing for

fruits that don't

       come to my

party :

       account for this

care

       taking time from our
       other taxonomies
       need to explain how this
       thought for my enemies'
       happy trails happens if
       we are enough in these
       numbers together

POSTSCRIPT

Most of the backstory isn't here, and that's because I don't know how to tell it, and I can't do it by myself. Still, there are two main facts to note:

1) My grandparents were in the U.S. Communist Party. That's no secret. My grandfather was also the President of Local 830, Retail and Wholesale Employees Union in New York City in the 1940s. He lost that position after he was subpoenaed to appear before the House of Representatives' Special Subcommittee to Investigate Communism in New York City Distributive Trades. He refused to answer "are you now or have you ever been," etc., as you've seen.

2) I also have in my possession a redacted copy of his FBI file, which he requested in the early 1970s after the passage of the Freedom of Information Act.

I've limited the information that I reveal about my grandparents to these forms of state documentation – that is, to these forms of state thinking, which are one portion of my inheritance, which is not the same thing as ancestry. I'm not filling in the story. I'm trying, instead, to think through the figure of the subcommittee as a form of kinship and as an organization of repression, so that the government (figured as, although never in fact, public) and some versions of the family form (figured as, although never in fact, private) are aligned by a variety of pseudo-dialectical sophistries. I did not invent these forms of thinking, but I tried to work in and around them. That is to say, I haven't made the choice here between negation and refusal. I hope, instead, that the objective situation will obviate the necessity to do so. Then, we will tell that story together, should we find it pleasing. Until then, here are some materials for shared activity.

ACKNOWLEDGMENTS

Some of these poems have appeared in earlier form in the following: the chapbook *Life of Riley* (2012, Bad Press), the co-authored collection *Viersomes #0* (2012, Veer Press, with Edmund Hardy, Danny Hayward, and slmendoza), and the print and electronic journals *Hi Zero, Infinite Editions, Olympia Monthly, Romulan Soup Woman,* and *Zone.*

Special thanks are due to Muffy Sunde, Yuisa Gimeno, Yolanda Alaniz, Christine Browning, Karla Alegria, Beatriz Paez, Luma Nichol, Toni Mendocino, Nellie Wong, Ryan Goodman, Mikel Wadewitz, Emma Heaney, Nisha Kunte, Mark Solomon, Judith Block Solomon, Sophie Robinson, Marianne Morris, Stephen Mooney, Juha Virtanen, Nell Perry, Joe Luna, Denise Riley, Barbara Galletly, Nat Raha, Adrienne Walser, Andrea Brady, Shaoling Ma, and many others for their varied versions of critique, support, and comradeship while I wrote this book between 2010 and 2015. Special thanks to Nina Solomon for letting me borrow Nat's file. Special thanks to Jasper Bernes, Joshua Clover, and Juliana Spahr; to Jasper in particular for his editorial, typesetting, and design work.